Wilbert Took a Walk

Written by Judy Spevack

Illustrated by Denise and Fernando

One day, Wilbert wanted to go for a walk.
He wanted to show off his new hat.

So he took his umbrella, put on his hat, and
began to walk.

The sun was out and it was a nice
day. Wilbert took off down the road.

Oh, no! Some clouds came and it began to rain.

Oh, good! Wilbert had an umbrella. He
opened his umbrella to keep the rain off his
new hat.

Oh, no! The wind began to blow. The wind
was so strong it blew him off his feet.

Oh, good! Wilbert could hold on to the
umbrella. But he took off in the wind.

8

Oh, no! The wind stopped. Wilbert began to
fall down.

Oh, good! Wilbert landed in a pile of hay.

Oh, no! The hay was in the back of a
truck! Wilbert knew they were going fast.

Oh, good! Two men were in the truck.

Oh, no! The two men could not hear
Wilbert.

Oh, good! The truck began to slow down. The
men were stopping. Wilbert got off the truck.

Oh, no! Wilbert was lost.

Oh, good! There were maps on the wall.
A map could show him the way.

Oh, good! The sun began to come out
again. So Wilbert took a walk . . .

all the way home.